Managing Our Resources

Air
A resource our world depends on

Heinemann Library
Chicago, Illinois

Ian Graham

© 2005 Heinemann Library

a division of Reed Elsevier Inc.

Chicago, Illinois

Customer Service 888-454-2279

Visit our website at
www.heinemannlibrary.com

Designed by David Poole and
Paul Myerscough

Photo research by Melissa Allison and
Andrea Sadler

Originated by Ambassador Litho Ltd.
Printed in China by WKT Company Limited

09 08 07 06 05

10 9 8 7 6 5 4 3 2 1

**Library of Congress Cataloging-in-
Publication Data**
Graham, Ian, 1953-
  Air : a resource our world depends on / Ian
Graham.
      p. cm. -- (Managing our resources)
  Includes bibliographical references and
index.
  ISBN 1-4034-5614-3 (lib. bdg.) --
  ISBN 1-4034-5622-4 (pbk.)
  1. Air--Juvenile literature. 2. Air--Pollution-
-Juvenile literature. I. Title.
  QC161.2.G73 2005
  551.5--dc22
                          2004005833

Acknowledgments
The author and publisher are grateful to the
following for permission to reproduce
copyright material: p. 5 top Taxi/Getty
Images; pp. 5 bottom, 9 top Harcourt
Education Ltd.; p. 6 Tim Kiusalaas/Corbis;
p. 7 Hans Dieter Brandl/FLPA; p.8 Andres
Stapff/Reuters; p. 9 bottom Tony
Hutchings/Getty Images; p. 10 Gavin
Rowell/Corbis; p. 11 Photri/Topham
Picturepoint; pp. 12, 17 Jim Sugar/Corbis;
pp. 13, 29 PA Photos; p. 14 Liz
Somerville/Photofusion; p. 15 top BBC
Natural History Unit; pp. 16, 22, 25, 27
ImageWorks/Topham Picturepoint; p. 18
Photodisc/Getty Images; p. 19 top, 19
bottom Charles O'Rear/Corbis; pp. 20, 21
Ralph White/Corbis; p. 23 W.
Wisniewski/FLPA; p. 24 (Adam Hart-
Davis/Science Photo Library; p. 26 bottom
Corbis; p. 28 Topham Picturepoint.

Cover photograph: Corbis/James Marshall

Contents

Some words are shown in bold, **like this.** You can find out what they mean by looking in the glossary.

What Is Air?

Air is all around you. It is what you breathe. When you feel the wind against your face, air is blowing on your skin.

Air is a mixture of different **gases**. Most of the air around you is made of a gas called nitrogen. Oxygen makes up one-fifth of the air. All of the gases in the air are mixed together.

What are clouds?

Air also contains some water **vapor,** which is water in the form of a gas. If this moisture cools down, it changes into tiny droplets of water. We see them as clouds. When the droplets are very small, they float in the air. Bigger droplets are too heavy to stay up in the sky, and they fall as rain. If they are cold enough, the droplets freeze and change into ice. These may fall as snow or hail.

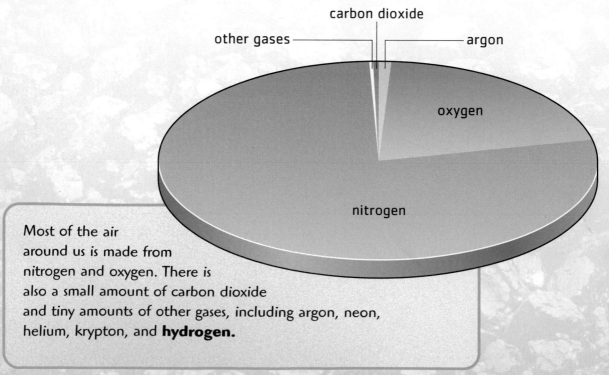

other gases — carbon dioxide — argon

oxygen

nitrogen

Most of the air around us is made from nitrogen and oxygen. There is also a small amount of carbon dioxide and tiny amounts of other gases, including argon, neon, helium, krypton, and **hydrogen.**

What is air pollution?

In some places, air contains extra gases and **smoke**. These are produced by factories, vehicles, and other things such as forest fires and **volcanoes**. We call these extra gases and smoke in the air **pollution**. Most pollution is bad for your health. Air pollution is usually worse in cities because there are more cars and factories there.

You cannot see air, but you can see its effect on things. Moving air can make a toy windmill spin.

Did you know?

A fluffy summer cloud that is 0.6 mile (one **kilometer**) in height, width, and length contains about 500 tons of water!

Clouds are made of water droplets so small that they float in the sky. It takes one million droplets to make one raindrop!

Why Is Air Important?

Air is needed by most living things on Earth. Most plants and animals take in air, use the oxygen in it, and give out another **gas,** carbon dioxide. Using air like this is called respiration. Animals respire by breathing. Green plants also need air, which they take in through their leaves.

How does air protect us?

The Sun gives out some harmful rays as well as sunlight and heat, which we need. If the harmful rays were to reach us on the ground, they would damage our skin and eyes. But the air around Earth stops them. It soaks up the most harmful rays before they reach us, but lets the sunlight and heat pass through.

We have to breathe air to stay alive. If this swimmer did not come up for air, he would probably drown.

How does air affect the temperature on Earth?

Without air, the temperature on the daylight side of Earth would soar to 212 °F (100 °C)—hot enough to boil water! As soon as the Sun set in the evening, the temperature would quickly drop to –238 °F (–150 °C). That is many times colder than ice! Air helps to spread the Sun's heat more evenly around Earth. It does the same thing in our homes. It helps to spread heat from fires and radiators through the rooms.

Death Valley, California, is the hottest place in the United States. The ground can be as hot as 201 °F (93.9 °C). It would be even hotter if there was no air blowing across it, carrying some of the heat away.

Did you know?

The Moon has no air to spread the Sun's heat around it. If you could stand on the Moon with one foot in shadow and one in sunlight, one foot would freeze while the other roasted!

Where does the wind come from?

When air warms up, it **expands,** or spreads itself out more thinly. It becomes lighter than the cold air around it and floats upward. When warm air cools, it sinks back toward the ground. All over Earth, air is rising in some places and falling in other places. As it rises and falls, Earth is turning beneath it. All of these movements stir up the air and help to create our weather.

How does wind help plants?

Some plants produce seeds so light that they can be blown around by the wind. This enables them to find new places to grow. Without the wind to carry them away, many seeds would drop next to their parent plants. As all these seeds and plants grew, they would take food, water, and light from each other. They would probably not grow well.

Moving air can be amazingly powerful and destructive. It can blow people and trees over and flatten buildings. Tropical storms called hurricanes and typhoons make winds that blow at more than 75 miles (120 kilometers) per hour—as fast as a car. Tornadoes are funnels of air that spin at speeds of up to 300 miles (500 kilometers) per hour.

Why is air needed for something to burn?

When something burns, it combines with oxygen in the air and gives out light and heat in the form of a flame. Without oxygen, it would not burn. So one way to put out a fire is to cover it, so it is not exposed to oxygen. Some fire extinguishers work by smothering a fire with foam, powder, or carbon dioxide **gas,** cutting off its supply of oxygen from the air.

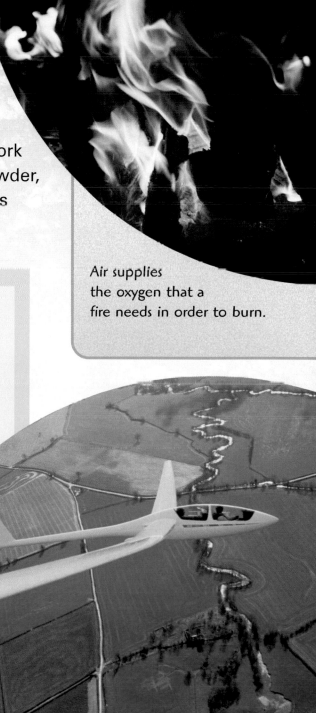

Air supplies the oxygen that a fire needs in order to burn.

Did you know?

Rising columns of warm air are called thermals. Glider pilots look for thermals. The rising air carries the glider up with it. A glider can climb thousands of feet high in this way.

Gliders rely on rising air to climb higher.

Where Is Air Found?

Air is found all around Earth. The air surrounding Earth is known as the **atmosphere**. From space, it looks like a thin, blue haze clinging to Earth.

The lowest part of the atmosphere is where clouds and weather form and where commercial jets fly. Higher up, the air gradually thins out. It becomes thinner and thinner until, about 90 miles (150 **kilometers**) above Earth, there is no air left.

Is air the same everywhere?

The force of gravity that pulls us down to Earth pulls air downward, too. Because of this, air is denser near the ground and thinner higher up.

Air is so thin at the top of a high mountain that mountaineers have to breathe extra oxygen through a mask.

At the top of a high mountain, there is so little air that it is difficult to breathe. Mountaineers who climb the highest mountains usually take extra oxygen with them to help them breathe.

Do all planets have an atmosphere?

Most planets have atmospheres, but they are not the same as Earth's. Venus has a very thick atmosphere made mainly of carbon dioxide. The giant planet Jupiter has an atmosphere mostly made of **hydrogen** and helium. If you were to go to another planet with a different atmosphere, you would not be able to breathe.

There is no air in space. Astronauts have to take their own atmospheres with them, in spacecraft or inside spacesuits.

Did you know?

If all the air around Earth was collected together and put on a scale, it would weigh about 4,500 billion tons.

What Can We Do to Air?

We can do many things to air to change the way it looks or how it can be used. We can heat it or cool it, we can squash it and turn it into a liquid, or we can clean it.

One of the simplest ways to process air is to heat it or cool it. If air is made very cold and squashed, it turns into a liquid. The different substances in liquid air boil at different temperatures. We can use this to separate out the different **gases** in air. If liquid air is allowed to warm up slowly, the nitrogen in it boils first and changes into a gas that can be collected. Liquid argon boils next and changes into a gas, and then oxygen boils. In this way, all the gases can eventually be separated.

The gases in air can be changed to liquids. This scientist is pouring liquid nitrogen.

Can we clean air?

Air can be cleaned using chemicals. If we keep breathing the same air, we use up the oxygen in it. Very soon, there is not enough oxygen left to breathe. In submarines, the air exhaled by the crew is treated with chemicals to remove the carbon dioxide. Filters also remove any hair and particles of dirt that are in the air. Then, with a little fresh oxygen added, the air can be breathed again.

Life support systems supply oxygen and remove carbon dioxide from the air on the International Space Station.

Did you know?

When some gas is changed into a liquid, the liquid takes up far less space than the gas. If about 28 cubic feet (800 liters) of ordinary air is changed into liquid air, it shrinks so much that it takes up only 0.04 cubic feet (1 liter) of space.

What Is Air Used For?

Air is used for heating, cooling, drying, and inflating things. Pool toys, life jackets, soccer balls, and car tires get their springiness from the air inside them. The air is squashed inside them so tightly that it pushes outward in all directions. This pushing is also called pressure.

If air is forced through a pipe by a pump, it can do work. Some tools, including jackhammers, work by pumped air. An air-powered drill is also called a pneumatic drill.

Air is lighter than water, so things filled with air float. Inflatable boats are made from a rubber tube filled with air.

How does air cool things down?

When cool air blows over something hot, the air soaks up the heat and carries it away. Computers use air to keep cool. A fan sucks in cool air and blows it over the hot parts inside.

Air-filled tires make a bicycle more comfortable to ride. The springiness of the air lessens the shock of some of the bumps on the ground.

Did you know?

Birds keep warm by fluffing out their feathers to trap air next to their skin.

How does air keep us warm?

Heat always tries to flow from hot to cold, like water flowing downhill. The heat inside a hot house tries to flow to the cold outside. One way to stop this is to have double-glazed windows. This means the windows have two panes of glass instead of one, with a space between them. The air in the space acts like insulation, keeping heat inside the house.

How is hot air useful?

Hot air warms things up and dries wet things. When the air in a room is warmed by a heater, it moves around, spreading the warmth to everything it touches. When you have wet hair you can blow it dry with a hair dryer. The hot air from the dryer heats the water on your hair. Then the water changes into a **vapor** and blows away.

A bear's fur traps a layer of warm air next to its skin and helps the bear stay warm.

space filled with air or argon gas

glass outside

glass inside

The air space in double-glazed windows helps to stop heat from leaking out. Sometimes the space is filled with argon **gas** instead of air, because it is even better for preventing heat loss.

How do engines use air?

Most cars, ships, and trains move because of what they do to air. They burn fuel to heat up the air inside an engine. Heating air makes it **expand**. Air spreads out and takes up more space. When air does this, it pushes with enough force to move parts of the engine. These moving parts are linked to the vehicle's wheels or propellers and make them turn.

What makes a jet engine go?

Jet engines use the power of hot air, too, but they work differently from car engines. A big fan at the front of the engine spins and sucks air inside. Some of the air is pushed and squeezed into the middle of the engine, where fuel is burned. The air heats up, expands, and rushes out of the back of the engine as a fast, fiery jet. Instead of turning wheels or propellers, it is this jet of air that pushes a jet airliner forward.

An airliner weighing hundreds of tons can be pushed through the sky by the force of hot air!

CASE STUDY:
Altamont Pass Wind Farm, California

Wind has energy that can be used to do work. A breeze can turn a toy windmill. A stronger wind can turn a bigger windmill. The windmill's spinning blades drive a generator that produces electricity.

What is a wind farm?

Machines that make electricity from the wind are called wind turbines. A small wind turbine can make electricity for just one house. A large group of much bigger wind turbines can make enough electricity for a whole town. Groups of wind turbines are called wind farms. The world's biggest wind farm is at Altamont Pass, near San Francisco, California. It has more than 7,000 wind turbines.

There are more wind turbines at Altamont Pass Wind Farm than at any other wind farm.

What Are the Gases in Air Used For?

Oxygen is one of the most useful **gases** in air. If oxygen is mixed with acetylene (another gas), it burns with a flame that is hot enough to melt metal. When two pieces of metal are held together and melted where they touch, they flow into each other. As they cool down and become hard, the two pieces are joined very strongly. Joining parts in this way is called welding.

Hydrogen is another very useful gas in air. It can be burned in an engine or used to make chemicals. Most of the hydrogen used in factories is extracted from natural gas or water.

Nitrogen is used to make some of the chemicals needed by factories. A lot of chemicals contain nitrogen. One of them is ammonia. Ammonia is used to make plant food, some household cleaners, and some plastics.

Did you know?

Helium extracted from air is lighter than air, so balloons filled with helium float upward.

Why is carbon dioxide special?

When most substances are heated, they change from a solid into a liquid and then into a gas. Carbon dioxide is different. Solid carbon dioxide changes into a gas without becoming a liquid first. Solid carbon dioxide looks like ice but contains no water, so it is also called dry ice. It is used to keep things cold.

Why do some gases glow?

Neon extracted from air is used in signs that light up shops. When electricity flows through a glass tube filled with neon, the neon gas glows red. Neon tubes are made in different shapes to spell names or make pictures. Other gases are used to make different colors.

The bubbles of gas that appear in a soft drink are made from carbon dioxide.

Neon signs help light cities and add beautiful colors to the skyline.

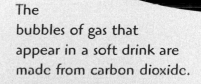

How Is Air Transported?

Air, or any of the **gases** it contains, can be pumped through pipes or hoses to move the air from one place to another. It can also be stored or transported by filling up **tanks**. A tank with a lot of air, or any other gas, inside it is said to be pressurized.

How do divers breathe underwater?

Most divers breathe air from tanks on their backs. Some divers do not wear air tanks. Instead, they breathe air pumped down from a boat through a hose. These divers can move around more easily without big, heavy tanks on their backs. They can also stay underwater longer. Divers with air tanks on their backs can stay underwater only for as long as the air in their tanks lasts.

Scuba divers breathe air from tanks on their backs. The word *scuba* stands for "self-contained underwater breathing apparatus."

CASE STUDY: Alvin

Alvin is a kind of small submarine called a **submersible**. In 1986 a crew guided Alvin 13,000 feet (3,960 meters) down into the Atlantic Ocean to explore the wreck of the passenger ship *Titanic*, which sank in 1912. Alvin was one of very few submersibles in the world that could dive so deep without being crushed by the water pressure around it. Alvin's crews use up the air inside it very quickly, so extra oxygen is carried in **tanks** for them to breathe.

How long does Alvin's air last?

Alvin has four oxygen tanks. Less than one tank is used during a normal dive, lasting a few hours. The four tanks contain enough oxygen for its usual crew of three people to breathe for three days.

Alvin supplies its crew with oxygen to breathe while the ship is underwater.

Will Air Ever Run Out?

Air will not run out because it is never completely used up. It is constantly **recycled** by plants and animals. Although air cannot run out, it can change. The amounts of the different **gases** in air can change. Air can also be changed by **pollution**. If air becomes very badly polluted all over the world, we could run out of enough clean air to breathe.

Has the air always been the same?

Air was different in the past. Before there were any plants on Earth, there was no oxygen in the **atmosphere.** It was locked up inside other chemicals. Plants changed the atmosphere by unlocking the oxygen and letting it go into the air. Trees and other plants are still doing this today.

The erupting Popocatepetl **volcano** in Mexico (shown here in 2000) poured out enormous amounts of gas. However, the atmosphere is so big that the volcano's gases were similar to a few drops of ink poured into a bathtub full of water.

How can the air be changed?

When plants die and rot, or when they burn, they give off carbon dioxide. Millions upon millions of trees and other plants would have to die or catch fire at the same time to change the air all around the world. Only an enormous disaster affecting the whole planet could do this, such as if a giant asteroid (a rock that falls from space) crashed into Earth.

How are people changing the air today?

Some of the things that people do can affect the atmosphere. Vehicles and factories pollute the air with **smoke** and gases. Fires used to clear land and burn old crops send smoke and carbon dioxide into the air. When fires were started in Indonesia in 1997, they spread out of control. Smoke covered Indonesia and several other countries. It even reached Australia!

Forests recycle gases in the Earth's atmosphere. During the day, plant leaves absorb carbon dioxide and give out oxygen. At night, they do the opposite.

Why Should We Take Care of the Air?

It is important to take care of the air because we cannot do without it. Some factories produce **smoke** and **gases** that change the natural balance of the gases in air. Some of them are harmless, but others can make it harder to breathe. Some of them are poisonous or cause diseases such as **cancer**. It is important to reduce air **pollution** as much as possible and to keep air clean.

Why is air pollution such a serious problem?

Air pollution does not stay in one place. Wind can blow it a long way so that it affects other places.

Buildings in big cities have to be cleaned because air pollution from traffic, factories, and fires settles on them and makes them dirty.

Smoke and **fumes** from factories in one country can blow over another country. The gases may mix with moisture in the air and form **acids**. When these acids fall as rain, they can kill forests and damage buildings.

Is air pollution getting better or worse?

There are more factories and cars today than ever before. However, many cities have cleaner air now than they had 100 years ago. At that time, many people heated their homes by burning coal, which produced thick black smoke. Sometimes, this smoke mixed with **fog** to make a choking mixture called smog. Today, air is cleaner because few people burn coal, factories are not allowed to pour smoke and fumes into the air, and vehicles have cleaner engines.

Did you know?

Mexico City is one of the world's most polluted cities. One reason for this is because the city is surrounded by mountains that stop the wind from blowing away the pollution.

CASE STUDY: Global Warming

Some **gases** are called **greenhouse gases** because they soak up heat from the Sun, like a greenhouse. Greenhouse gases include carbon dioxide and methane. If the **atmosphere** contains more of these gases, it traps more heat and warms up. This is called **global warming** because it affects the whole world.

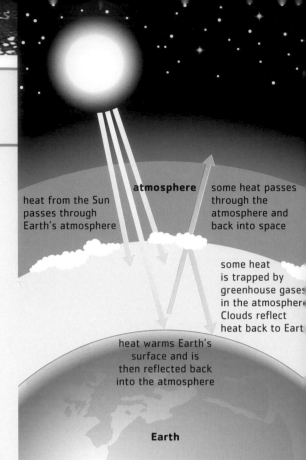

atmosphere

heat from the Sun passes through Earth's atmosphere

some heat passes through the atmosphere and back into space

some heat is trapped by greenhouse gases in the atmosphere. Clouds reflect heat back to Earth

heat warms Earth's surface and is then reflected back into the atmosphere

Earth

Greenhouse gases trap heat from the Sun and stop it from escaping into space.

Why is global warming bad for us?

A warmer atmosphere changes our weather. Most scientists believe this is happening now. The gases produced by factories and traffic may be warming the atmosphere and making storms, floods, and **droughts** worse.

Did you know?

Nearly half of the greenhouse gases produced by New Zealand come from its 50 million sheep burping!

How Can We Take Care of the Air?

There are several ways of protecting the air. We can look for ways of reducing air **pollution.** We can also protect the world's great forests, such as the Amazon rain forest in South America, so that they carry on **recycling** the air and producing fresh oxygen.

How can we reduce air pollution?

One way of reducing air pollution is to change to cleaner ways of making electricity. Making electricity from the wind produces less pollution than burning coal or oil. Another way to reduce pollution is to use less electricity. We could make our homes less drafty so that we need less energy to heat them. We could also use lights, washing machines, and refrigerators that are designed to use less electricity.

So many trees are cut down every year that it is important to plant more to replace them.

How can we make traffic less polluting?

We could make fewer trips by car, perhaps by using public transportation whenever possible. Carmakers could design engines that produce less **pollution**. We could use engines that burn cleaner fuels, such as **hydrogen**. When hydrogen burns, the main thing that is produced as a result of the process is water.

How do factories reduce air pollution?

In many countries, factories are not allowed to send all the **smoke** and waste **gases** they produce up chimneys into the air. The chimneys are fitted with filters that trap most of the sooty particles in the smoke. The smoke is also sometimes treated with chemicals to remove harmful gases.

Small boxes attached to poles in many towns and cities today are used to check how clean the air is.

CASE STUDY:
The Kyoto Treaty

Governments meet regularly to discuss how the land, sea, and air are affected by what people do. They decide what should be done to protect Earth. In 1997 governments met in Kyoto, Japan, to decide what to do about **global warming**. They decided to cut the amount of **greenhouse gases** that countries produce. Their agreement is called the Kyoto **Treaty**.

Is the Kyoto Treaty working?

In 2001 some countries were unhappy with the Kyoto Treaty. It forced their power plants and factories to burn less coal and oil. Poorer countries trying to provide more power, water, and transportation need more electricity and vehicles, but these would produce more greenhouse gases. It is harder for these countries to stick to the treaty. After more discussion, 180 countries agreed that some countries should reduce their greenhouse gases more than others.

Canadian Prime Minister Jean Chrétien is shown here signing the Kyoto Treaty.

Glossary

acid chemical compound that contains hydrogen and usually dissolves in water. Weak acids have a sour taste. Strong acids eat into other materials. Oranges and lemons contain citric acid. Your stomach contains acid to help digest food.

atmosphere mixture of gases that surrounds a planet or a moon in space

cancer disease that involves a tumor spreading to parts of the body and that usually causes death if not treated

drought long period of time when there is no rain, leaving the ground too dry to grow plants. A drought can last for a few weeks, months, or even years.

expand to increase in size, number, or amount. When a gas expands, it fills a bigger space.

fume harmful or unpleasant gas, smoke, or vapor

gas substance that has no set shape and that expands without limit. Nitrogen and oxygen are the main gases in air.

global warming increase in the average surface temperature of Earth, due to an increase in certain gases, such as carbon dioxide, in the atmosphere

greenhouse gas substance that absorbs heat from the Sun and helps to warm the atmosphere and Earth. This warming is called the greenhouse effect.

hydrogen chemical element that is found in nature as a flammable, colorless, and odorless gas

pollution harmful or poisonous substances in nature, usually produced by the activities of humans

recycle to process for reuse instead of using materials only once and then throwing them away

submersible small submarine. Submersibles cannot be piloted very far on their own. They have to be carried on a ship to the place where they are used to dive into bodies of water.

tank container for holding liquids or gases

treaty agreement signed between two or more countries

vapor fine particles of matter that float in and cloud the air

volcano vent, or hole, in Earth's crust from which melted or hot rock and steam come out

More Books to Read

Ballard, Carol. *Solids, Liquids, and Gases: From Air to Stone.* Chicago: Heinemann Library, 2003.

Chambers, Catherine. *Tornadoes.* Chicago: Heinemann Library, 2000.

Murphy, Bryan. *Experiment With Air.* Chanhassen, Minn.: Creative Publishing, 2004.

Rodgers, Alan, and Angella Streluk. *Wind and Air Pressure.* Chicago: Heinemann Library, 2002.

Stewart, Melissa. *Air Is Everywhere.* Minneapolis, Minn.: Compass Point Books, 2004.

Stille, Darlene. *Air: Outside, Inside, and All Around.* Minneapolis, Minn.: Picture Window Books, 2004.

Tocci, Salvatore. *Experiments with Air.* Danbury, Conn.: Scholastic Library, 2003.

Trapp, Clayton. *Polluted Air.* Chicago: Raintree, 2004.

Index